PREHISTORIC WORLD

JURASSIC LIFE

Dougal Dixon

BARRON'S

First edition for the United States, its territories and dependencies, Canada, and
the Philippine Republic published in 2006 by Barron's Educational Series, Inc.

Copyright © 2006 *ticktock* Entertainment Ltd. First published in Great Britain by ticktock Media Ltd.

All inquiries should be addressed to:
Barron's Educational Series, Inc.
250 Wireless Blvd.
Hauppauge, New York 11788
www.barronseduc.com

Library of Congress Control Number: 2005938244

ISBN-13: 978-0-7641-3478-4
ISBN-10: 0-7641-3478-7

Printed in China
9 8 7 6 5 4 3 2 1

CONTENTS

INTRODUCTION

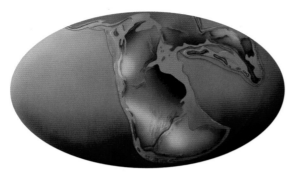

This map shows how the Earth looked in the Jurassic Period. During this period, Earth was mostly deserts. By the end of this period the continents were splitting up.

This map shows how the Earth looks today. See how different it looks? The continents have completely changed around.

Prehistoric World is a series of six books about the evolution of animals.

The Earth's history is divided into sections called eras. Each era is divided into periods which are millions of years long.

This book looks at the Jurassic Period when dinosaurs reached their hugest sizes. The dinosaurs came in all shapes and sizes. Some were as small as foxes, others were bigger than modern whales. Inside this book are the most incredible of these animals.

PREHISTORIC WORLD TIMELINE

Use this timeline to trace prehistoric life. It shows how simple creatures evolved into more diverse forms. This took millions and millions of years. That is what MYA stands for – millions of years ago.

	BOOK	PERIOD	
CENOZOIC ERA	**THE ICE AGE**	1.75 MYA to now QUATERNARY	*This is a period of ice ages and mammals. Our direct relatives, Homo sapiens, also appear.*
	ANCIENT MAMMALS	65 to 1.75 MYA TERTIARY	*The first mammals and giant, hunting birds first became important in this period. Our first human relatives also start to evolve.*
MESOZOIC ERA	**CRETACEOUS LIFE**	135 to 65 MYA CRETACEOUS	*Huge dinosaurs evolve. They all die by the end of this period.*
	JURASSIC LIFE	203 to 135 MYA JURASSIC	*Large and small dinosaurs and flying creatures develop.*
	TRIASSIC LIFE	250 to 203 MYA TRIASSIC	*The "Age of the Dinosaurs" begins.*
PALEOZIC ERA	**EARLY LIFE**	295 to 250 MYA PERMIAN	*Sail-backed reptiles start to appear.*
		355 to 295 MYA CARBONIFEROUS	*The first reptiles appear, and tropical forests develop.*
		410 to 355 MYA DEVONIAN	*Bony fish evolve. Trees and insects appear.*
		435 to 410 MYA SILURIAN	*Fish with jaws develop, and land creatures appear.*
		500 to 435 MYA ORDOVICIAN	*Primitive fishes, trilobites, shellfish, and plants evolve.*
		540 to 500 MYA CAMBRIAN	*First animals with skeletons appear.*

*I*CHTHYOSAURUS

In the Mesozoic Era, the seas were full of swimming reptiles. One of the most common were the ichthyosaurs, or "fish-lizards." When they first evolved, ichthyosaurs were big whale-like animals. By the time of the Jurassic Period, the ichthyosaurs, including *Ichthyosaurus* itself, were smaller and more dolphin-like.

Ichthyosaurs gave birth to live young. They did not need to come ashore to lay eggs. We know this because there are fossils of baby ichthyosaurs preserved while actually emerging from their mother's body.

Ichthyosaurus and the other ichthyosaurs were the fastest hunters in the Jurassic seas. Like modern dolphins they could chase and catch the fastest of the fish and squid-like animals that lived at the time.

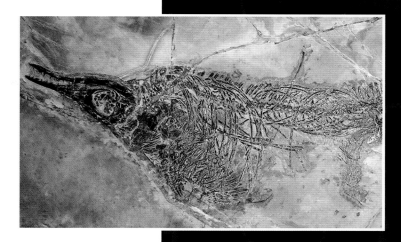

ANIMAL
FACTFILE

NAME: *Ichthyosaurus* (fish lizard)

PRONOUNCED: ik-thee-oh-sawr-us

GROUP: Ichthyosaur

WHERE IT LIVED: Worldwide

WHEN IT LIVED: Early Jurassic period (208 to 178 million years ago)

LENGTH: 7 feet (2 meters)

SPECIAL FEATURES: Most streamlined and fish-like of the reptiles

FOOD: Fish and cephalopods

MAIN ENEMY: Pliosaurs

DID YOU KNOW?: Usually we do not know what the soft fleshy parts of a fossil animal look like, but some fossils of *Ichthyosaurus* still have their fins preserved.

CRYPTOCLIDUS

The plesiosaurs were one of the most important swimming reptiles of Jurassic times. There were two types – those with long necks and those with short necks. *Cryptoclidus* was a long-necked plesiosaur.

"Like a snake threaded through a turtle" was the description of a long-necked plesiosaur given by one early paleontologist. The long neck, the broad body, and the paddles give this impression.

Cryptoclidus moved through the water with a flying action, with the front paddles working like wings, and the hind paddles as stabilizers. It could reach around for food with its long neck.

ANIMAL FACTFILE

NAME: *Cryptoclidus* (hidden collar bone)

PRONOUNCED: crip-tow-cly-dus

GROUP: Long-necked plesiosaurs

WHERE IT LIVED: Europe

WHEN IT LIVED: Late Jurassic Period (165 to 150 million years ago)

LENGTH: 26 feet (8 meters)

SPECIAL FEATURES: Long pointed teeth ideal for catching slippery prey

FOOD: Fish and squid

MAIN ENEMY: Short-necked plesiosaurs, such as *Liopleurodon*

DID YOU KNOW?: Fossils form more easily in the sea than on land, so fossils from swimming reptiles are more common than fossils from some land animals. Scientists were studying plesiosaur fossils long before they disovered dinosaur fossils.

*L*IOPLEURODON

The biggest reptiles of the Jurassic seas,
and probably the biggest meat-eating
animals of all time, were the
pliosaurs. They had short
necks and very long jaws.
The biggest of these
was the huge
Liopleurodon.

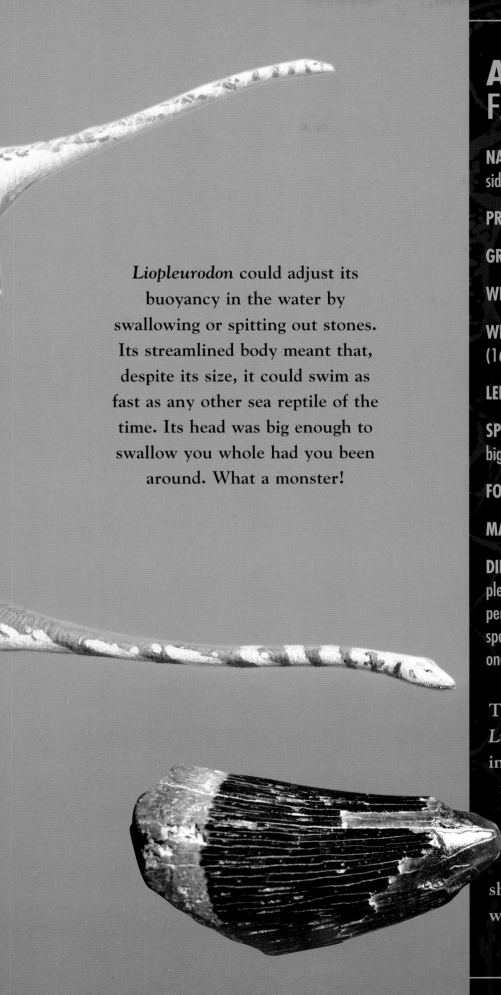

Liopleurodon could adjust its buoyancy in the water by swallowing or spitting out stones. Its streamlined body meant that, despite its size, it could swim as fast as any other sea reptile of the time. Its head was big enough to swallow you whole had you been around. What a monster!

This is the tooth of a *Liopleurodon*. It is about 8 inches (20 cm) long. Bite marks from *Liopleurodon* have been found on the bones of ichthyosaurs and other plesiosaurs, showing that *Liopleurodon* was a fearsome predator.

PTERODACTYLUS

The skies were full of flying animals in late Jurassic times, including insects and the first birds. However, the most important flying animals were reptiles, the pterosaurs. There were two groups, the long-tailed pterosaurs and the short-tailed pterosaurs. *Pterodactylus* was a short-tailed pterosaur.

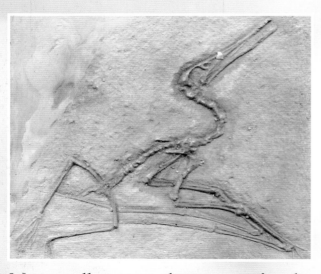

Many well-preserved pterosaur fossils have been found. Here you can clearly see the bones of the spine and neck. In some fossils, it is even possible to see the wing membrane.

ANIMAL
FACTFILE

NAME: *Pterodactylus* (wing finger)

PRONOUNCED: ter-oh-dak-til-us

GROUP: Pterodactyloid – the short-tailed pterosaurs

WHERE IT LIVED: Northern Europe and Africa

WHEN IT LIVED: Late Jurassic Period (157 to 146 million years ago)

WINGSPAN: 3 feet (1 meter)

SPECIAL FEATURES: Broad wings, a short tail and a long neck

FOOD: Fish and small reptiles

MAIN ENEMY: Larger pterosaurs

DID YOU KNOW?: The first pterosaurs found were thought to have been swimming animals – scientists thought that the wings were fins.

The common name "pterodactyl" is used for the whole of the pterosaur group. Scientifically, though, it should only be used for the *Pterodactylus* group. There were many different sizes and shapes of pterosaur at that time.

CAMPTOSAURUS

Camptosaurus was one of the two-footed plant-eating dinosaurs. They spent most of their time on hind legs and could reach up into the branches of trees to find their food. However, the bigger individuals were too heavy to spend much of their time on hind legs and must have moved around on all fours.

Camptosaurus lived in the thick riverside forests. It probably lived in herds like many plant-eating animals today. This would have given them some protection against the big meat-eaters of the time.

Camptosaurus and its relatives had cheeks like we have. This meant they could hold their food in their mouth to chew it before swallowing. It made digesting food easier. The plant-eating dinosaurs with long necks swallowed their food right away.

ANIMAL FACTFILE

NAME: *Camptosaurus* (flexible lizard)

PRONOUNCED: camp-toh-sawr-us

GROUP: Ornithopod dinosaur

WHERE IT LIVED: Western United States

WHEN IT LIVED: Late Jurassic Period (156 to 145 million years ago)

LENGTH: 23 feet (7 meters)

SPECIAL FEATURES: Small head with a strong beak at the front and lots of little grinding teeth at the back

FOOD: Low-growing plants

MAIN ENEMY: Big meat-eating dinosaurs like *Allosaurus*

DID YOU KNOW?: Good skeletons of *Camptosaurus* have been known since the 1880s.

HETERODONTOSAURUS

Look at this! Big fierce teeth. Grasping claws. Aggressive pose. It must be a ferocious meat-eater! Wrong. *Heterodontosaurus* was a plant-eating dinosaur that probably scared away its enemies by putting on a show. If that did not work, it was small and light enough to run away quickly.

This skull of *Heterodontosaurus* is one of the best-preserved fossil dinosaur skulls known. It was found in South Africa in 1966. The complete skeleton of *Heterodontosaurus* shows that it had long running hind legs, and its short arms had little hands for grasping.

ANIMAL
FACTFILE

NAME: *Heterodontosaurus* (lizard with differently-shaped teeth)

PRONOUNCED: het-er-oh-don-toh-sawr-us

GROUP: Ornithopod dinosaur

WHERE IT LIVED: South Africa

WHEN IT LIVED: Early Jurassic Period (208 to 200 million years ago)

LENGTH: 4 feet (1.2 meters)

SPECIAL FEATURES: Three kinds of teeth – nipping teeth inside the beak at the front, tusks at the side, and grinding teeth at the back

FOOD: Plants

MAIN ENEMY: Meat-eating dinosaurs and crocodiles

DID YOU KNOW?: *Heterodontosaurus* had five-fingered hands, but two of the fingers were tiny.

It is possible that only male *Heterodontosaurus* had the long side tusks. Maybe they were used for display during the mating season, to scare away rivals. Like other ornithopods, *Heterodontosaurus* had a bird-like beak at the front of the mouth.

SCUTELLOSAURUS

One of the earliest armored dinosaurs was *Scutellosaurus*. Its neck, back and long tail were covered in tiny armored shields and its legs were long and thin. In later periods, armored dinosaurs grew very big, but *Scutellosaurus* was only the size of a small dog.

Scutellosaurus could run on its hind legs, but the armor would have made it rather heavy. It would have spent most of its time on all fours.

Apart from the shields, *Scutellosaurus* was very similar to the two-footed plant-eating dinosaurs such as *Camptosaurus*. It shows that the armored dinosaurs evolved from this group.

ANIMAL
FACTFILE

NAME: *Scutellosaurus* (lizard with little shields)

PRONOUNCED: scoo-tel-oh-sawr-us

GROUP: Thyreophoran dinosaur

WHERE IT LIVED: United States

WHEN IT LIVED: Early Jurassic Period (208 to 200 million years ago)

LENGTH: 4 feet (1.2 meters), but most of this length was its tail

SPECIAL FEATURES: Covered in several kinds of armor, including oval plates along the side and a ridge of vertical plates down the back and tail

FOOD: Low-growing plants

MAIN ENEMY: Big meat-eating dinosaurs

DID YOU KNOW?: *Scutellosaurus* could defend itself with its armor and could also run away from danger. It was a stage in the evolution of armored dinosaurs from the earlier fast-running forms.

STEGOSAURUS

One of the most recognizable of the armored dinosaurs was *Stegosaurus*. It had a double row of plates down its back. These were either covered in horns and used for defense, or covered in skin and used to keep the dinosaur warm – we are not yet sure which.

Stegosaurus may have used its plates to keep warm. When it was cold it would have stood sideways to the sun, so sunlight could warm the plates. When *Stegosaurus* was hot it could have cooled itself off by holding the plates into the wind.

ANIMAL
FACTFILE

NAME: *Stegosaurus* (roofed lizard)

PRONOUNCED: steg-oh-sawr-us

GROUP: Thyreophoran dinosaur

WHERE IT LIVED: Midwestern United States

WHEN IT LIVED: Late Jurassic Period (156 to 140 million years ago)

LENGTH: 30 feet (9 meters)

SPECIAL FEATURES: Two pairs of spikes on tail for defense

FOOD: Plants

MAIN ENEMY: Big meat-eating dinosaurs like *Allosaurus*

DID YOU KNOW?: The brain of *Stegosaurus* is so small that people used to think it must have had a second brain in its hips to control the legs and tail.

Stegosaurus probably spent most of its time on four legs. However, its hips and hind legs were very strong, showing that it could rear up on its hind legs to eat from the low branches of trees.

BRACHIOSAURUS

One of the biggest dinosaurs was *Brachiosaurus*.
It was one of the long-necked plant-eating sauropods.
There were many types of big sauropods in the Late
Jurassic Period. Some were adapted for grazing the
plants that grew close to the ground. Others, like
Brachiosaurus, were tall so they could
eat the leaves and needles
from high trees.

Brachiosaurus!
One of the
biggest land-
living animals known! How on earth could it support that
great weight? In fact, the bones of *Brachiosaurus* weren't
as heavy as they look. They were hollow, which made
them extremely strong, but lightweight at the same time.

ANIMAL FACTFILE

NAME: *Brachiosaurus* (arm lizard)

PRONOUNCED: brack-ee-oh-sawr-us

GROUP: Sauropod dinosaur

WHERE IT LIVED: East Africa and the Midwestern United States

WHEN IT LIVED: Mid to Late Jurassic Period (160 to 145 million years ago)

LENGTH: 80 feet (24 meters)

SPECIAL FEATURES: Long neck, small head. The tail was 25 feet (8 meters) long — relatively short for a sauropod

FOOD: Leaves from trees

MAIN ENEMY: Big meat-eating dinosaurs like *Allosaurus*

DID YOU KNOW?: *Brachiosaurus* fossils have been found in both Africa and North America, showing that the two continents were close together in Late Jurassic times.

Can you picture how big *Brachiosaurus* was? This photo might help. *Brachiosaurus* was over 40 feet (12 meters) tall, about the height of a four-story building.

BRACHYTRACHELOPAN

Brachytrachelopan had the shortest neck of all sauropods. It had the usual number of vertebrae in its neck, but they were much shorter than the vertebrae in most sauropods. In fact *Brachytrachelopan* must have looked rather like a *Stegosaurus*, but without the plates. *Brachytrachelopan* also had a ridge down its back with spines on the top.

Brachytrachelopan had a high ridge down its back. This may have held the strong muscles needed to support the neck, or it may have been brightly colored and used for signaling to other dinosaurs – attracting them as mates or warning them to stay away.

Most sauropods, such as *Brachiosaurus,* had long necks that allowed them either to reach up into trees or to sweep around for low-growing plants. *Brachytrachelopan* must have concentrated on the plants growing on the ground immediately in front of it.

ANIMAL FACTFILE

NAME: *Brachytrachelopan* (short-necked shepherd god)

PRONOUNCED: brack-ee-track-el-oh-pan

GROUP: Sauropod dinosaur

WHERE IT LIVED: Argentina

WHEN IT LIVED: Late Jurassic Period (150 million years ago)

LENGTH: 25 feet (8 meters)

SPECIAL FEATURES: The sauropod with the shortest neck

FOOD: Low-growing plants

MAIN ENEMY: Big meat-eating dinosaurs

DID YOU KNOW?: Only half of one skeleton has ever been found. All we know of *Brachytrachelopan* comes from that.

ALLOSAURUS

One of the biggest and fiercest of the meat-eating dinosaurs in the Late Jurassic Period was *Allosaurus*. It was big enough to hunt the biggest of the plant-eating sauropods, although, like lions and tigers today, it probably concentrated on the young, the old, and the injured.

Over 40 skeletons of *Allosaurus* have been found in a single quarry in Utah. Most of the mounted *Allosaurus* skeletons that we see in museums today have come from this site.

With the big claws on its three-fingered hands, *Allosaurus* could seize its prey. It would then have killed it with its steak-knife teeth. After it had finished eating its prey, there would have been plenty left over for smaller scavenging dinosaurs and pterosaurs.

ANIMAL FACTFILE

NAME: *Allosaurus* (different lizard)

PRONOUNCED: al-oh-sawr-us

GROUP: Theropod dinosaur

WHERE IT LIVED: Western United States

WHEN IT LIVED: Late Jurassic Period (156 to 145 million years ago)

LENGTH: 38 feet (11.5 meters)

SPECIAL FEATURES: The biggest land-living meat-eater of the time

FOOD: Big plant-eating dinosaurs, like *Stegosaurus* or *Brachiosaurus*

MAIN ENEMY: None

DID YOU KNOW?: *Allosaurus* weighed 5 tons — about the weight of an elephant. There were several smaller species, some weighing as little as 1 ton.

GUANLONG

The most famous meat-eating dinosaur of all time must be *Tyrannosaurus*. *Guanlong* was an early relative. It was quite small considering the size of its relatives. But it was still a fierce hunter of smaller animals.

Most small active animals, like mammals and birds, are warm-blooded. Hair or feathers help them to control their body temperature. We think that the small meat-eating dinosaurs were active enough to have been warm blooded and so we think they probably had a feathery covering.

Fossils show that *Guanlong* had a crest on its head. This is something unusual among the tyrannosaurs. It would have been used for signaling to other dinosaurs.

ANIMAL FAMILIES GLOSSARY

Cephalopod — literally the "head-footed" animals. The modern types, the octopus and squid, seem to have legs branching from their faces. In prehistoric times many cephalopods had chambered shells.

Ichthyosaur — a group of sea-going reptiles. They were well-adapted to living in the sea, and looked like dolphins or sharks. They had fins on their tails and backs, and paddles for limbs. Ichthyosaurs were common in the Triassic and the Jurassic Periods but died out in the Cretaceous.

Ornithopod — the plant-eating dinosaur group that usually used two legs. They were present throughout the late Triassic and Jurassic Periods, but it was in the later Cretaceous that they became really important.

Plesiosaur — the group of swimming reptiles with the paddle-shaped limbs and flat bodies. There were two types — the long-necked type and the whale-like, short-necked type. They lived throughout dinosaur times.

Pterodactyloid — one of the two groups of pterosaurs. These had short tails and long necks, unlike the other group, the rhamphorhynchoids, that had long tails and short necks.

Pterosaur — the flying reptiles of the age of dinosaurs. They had broad leathery wings supported on a long fourth finger, and were covered in hair to keep them warm.

Sauropod — the plant-eating dinosaur group that had the huge bodies, the long necks, and the long tails. They were the biggest land-living animals that ever lived, and reached their peak in late Jurassic times.

Theropod — the meat-eating dinosaur group. They all had the same shape — long jaws with sharp teeth, long strong hind legs, smaller front legs with clawed hands, and a small body balanced by a long tail.

Thyreophoran — the armored dinosaur group. There were two main lines. The first to develop were the plated stegosaurs, and later came the armor-covered ankylosaurs.

Tyrannosaur — one of the theropod dinosaur groups. At the end of the Cretaceous Period they were among the biggest meat-eaters of all time, but the early forms, in the late Jurassic Period, were quite small animals.

LOSSARY

Adapted — changed to survive in a particular habitat or weather conditions.

Cephalopod — an animal that lives in the sea and which has a big head and tentacles, such as an octopus.

Continents — the world's main land masses such as Africa and Europe.

Evolution — changes or developments that happen to all forms of life over millions of years as a result of changes in the environment.

Evolve — to change or develop.

Fossil — the remains of a prehistoric plant or animal that has been buried for a long time and become hardened in rock.

Grinding teeth — these are teeth used to chew food.

Hollow bones — bones that have a space inside them so that they are not solid. Hollow bones are much lighter than solid bones.

Nipping teeth — these are teeth used to bite leaves off the trees.

Ornithopod — a type of plant-eating dinosaur.

Paleontologist — a scientist who studies fossils.

Plesiosaur — a reptile which lived in the sea.

Prey — animals that are hunted by other animals as food.

Quarry — a place where stones are dug up for building.

Sauropod — a large plant-eating dinosaur.

Spine — the backbone of an animal.

Stabilizers — something, such as a tail, which helps an animal to keep its balance.

Streamlined — an animal with a smooth, bullet-shaped body so that it can move through air or water easily and quickly.

Trilobite — an early type of sea animal that no longer exists.

Tyrannosaur — a type of large meat-eating dinosaur.

Vertebrae — small bones which help to form the spine.

Vertical plates — flat bones which stood upright on the back of some dinosaurs.

Warm-blooded — animals, such as small mammals, which always have the same body temperature.

Well-preserved fossil — a fossil which is in good condition.

Wing membrane — a thin sheet of skin attached to bone, which forms a wing.

INDEX

PICTURE CREDITS

T = top, B = bottom, R = right, L = left

Main image: 20-21, 26-27 Simon Mendez; 10-11
Bob Nicholls; 6-7, 8-9, 12-13, 14-15, 16-17, 18-19, 22-23, 24-25, 28-29 Luis Rey

4TL, 4TR, 5 (Cenozoic Era) 7, 9, 11, 12, 15, 20, 25, 26 Ticktock Media archive; 5 (Mesozoic Era top, Paleozoic Era top) Simon Mendez; 5 (Mesozoic Era center, Paleozoic Era bottom) Luis Rey; 5 (Mesozoic Era bottom) Lisa Alderson; 16 The Natural History Museum, London; 19 Chris Tomlin; 23 Louie Psihoyos/Corbis; 29 Tyler Olson/Shutterstock

Every effort has been made to trace the copyright holders and we apologize in advance for any unintentional omissions.
We would be pleased to insert the appropriate acknowledgment in any subsequent edition of this publication.